# Pocket Books

# Cities
## of the
# World

# Kane Miller
A DIVISION OF EDC PUBLISHING

D0829602

First American Edition 2016
Kane Miller, A Division of EDC Publishing

Copyright © Green Android Ltd 2016

For information contact:
Kane Miller, A Division of EDC Publishing
P.O. Box 470663
Tulsa, OK 74147-0663
**www.kanemiller.com**
**www.edcpub.com**
**www.usbornebooksandmore.com**

Please note that every effort has been made to check the accuracy of the information contained in this book, and to credit the copyright holders correctly. Green Android Ltd apologize for any unintentional errors or omissions, and would be happy to include revisions to content and/or acknowledgements in subsequent editions of this book.

Printed and bound in China, June 2016
Library of Congress Control Number: 2015947530
ISBN: 978-1-61067-472-0

Images © shutterstock.com: Copenhagen © S-F, Jakarta © saiko3p, Phnom Penh, Melbourne © Aleksandar Todorovic, Stockholm © Alexander Tolstykh, Sao Paulo © Alf Ribeiro, Montreal © Alphonse Tran, Jakarta © amadeustx, Las Vegas © Andrew Zarivny, Bangkok © anekoho, Oslo © Anna Jedynak, Karachi © arifkamalzaidi, Budapest © Artur Bogacki, Lisbon © ATGImages, Vatican City © Banauke, Lagos © Bill Kret, Tehran © Borna_Mirahmadian, Santiago © byvalet, Cairo © Bzzuspajk, Kuala Lumpur © Calvin Chan, Venice, Seattle © canadastock, Berlin © CCat82, bus (p3) © Chris Jenner, Lima © Christian Vinces, Guangzhou © chungking, seoul © CJ Nattanai, Macau © coloursinmylife, Osaka © cowardlion, Vancouver © Dan Breckwoldt, New York © David Persson, Dublin © David Soanes, Bogota © De Jongh Photography, Addis Ababa © Dereje, Philadelphia © f11photo, Riyadh © Fedor Selivanov, Accra © Felix Lipov, mexico city © Frontpage, Mexico City © Gerardo Borbolla, Dakar © Gil.K, Shanghai © Iakov Kalinin, Vienna © Jeff Whyte, Quito © Jess Kraft, Guadalajara © Jesus Cervantes, Miami © Jonathan G, New Orleans © Jorg Hackemann, Manila, Singapore © joyfull, central park © Kateryna Tsygankova, Edinburgh © kay roxby, Bucharest © kirych, San Francisco © kropic1, Freetown © LEONARDO VITI, Hong Kong, Tokyo© leungchopan, Dallas © Manamana, Honolulu © Martina Roth, Marrakech, Ljubljana © Matej Kastelic, Montevideo © Matyas Rehak, Buenos Aires © meunierd, Guatemala City © Milosz_M, Mexico City © Morenovel, Ankara © muratart, Sydney © Nadezda Zavitaeva, Warsaw © Nahlik, Sofia © Nataliya Nazarova, Barcelona © Natursports, Nairobi © Nick Fox, Bengaluru © Noppasin, Helsinki © Oleksiy Mark, Zagreb © OPIS Zagreb, Washington, D.C. © Orhan Cam, Hanoi © Palis Michalis, Seoul © Panya K, Managua © Pascal RATEAU, Tianjin © pavel dudek, Chicago © Pigprox, Zurich © Pocholo Calapre, Ho Chi Minh City © Prasit Rodphan, Rome © r.nagy, Kolkata, Mumbai © Radiokafka, Caracas © Rafael Martin-Gaitero, Baghdad © rasoulali, Reykjavik © RHIMAGE, Tallinn, Boston © Richard Cavalleri, Cape Town © Robyn Gwilt, Toronto © Ronald Sumners, Brussels © S-F, Paris, London © S.Borisov, New Delhi © saiko3p, Beijing, Chengdu, Nagoya, Taipei, Los Angeles © Sean Pavone, Istanbul © seregalsv, Agra © Serg Zastavkin, Mecca © shahreen, Hyderabad © SNEHIT, Dubai © Sophie James, Lahore © suronin, Rio de Janeiro © T photography, Athens © TakB, skyscrapers(p2), Tokyo, Belgrade © Tupungato, Johannesburg © tusharkoley, Tunis © Uta Scholl, Jerusalem © VanderWolf Images, Amsterdam © Veronika Galkina, St. Petersburg © vichie81, Wellington © Victor Maschek, Kiev © Vlada Z, Moscow © vvoe, Prague © Xiong Wei. Images © istock.com: Tegucigalpa © mtcurado, Delhi © LUKASZ-NOWAK1. Images © wikicommons :Santa Cruz de la Sierra © ACS, Kinshasa © Irene2005, Gaborone © US Army Africa, Dongguan © MichaelMichaelMichaels, Chennai © VtTN.

# Introducing cities

There are more than 4,400 cities in the world with populations in excess of 150,000 people. There are enormous metropolises, such as London, Tokyo and New York, that have populations in the many millions, and small cities of 100,000 residents. Currently, over half the world's population live within cities, and researchers believe that this percentage will rise over the next decades.

**Skyscrapers of over 40 stories dominate many city skylines**

**London's red double-decker buses transport people around the city**

**New York's Central Park offers city dwellers access to green spaces**

## Elements of a city

Buildings and housing are the most visible hallmarks of a city. City buildings are taller and more numerous and closely spaced than those in towns or rural areas.

Cities also need to have transportation systems so people can get to work, to shops, services and schools. Many cities have extensive public transportation systems, with buses, trains, trams, ferries and underground railways.

Green spaces and plazas (squares) provide recreational areas so that citizens can escape the hustle and bustle of city life.

# How to use this book

This book gives you key features and informative profiles of 118 cities around the world.

Continent

Country

Factfile
(see opposite page)

**Cities of the world**

Asia

India

Kolkata — City name

Color photograph

**Factfile**

| | |
|---|---|
| Population | 14,667,000 |
| Land area | 465 square miles |
| Density | 31,500 people per square mile |
| Languages | Bengali, English and Urdu (official) and Hindi |
| Currency | Indian rupee |
| Temperature | 96.7 °F (high) / 57.6 °F (low) |

**Hot spot** The Calcutta Football League, started in 1898, is one of the oldest leagues in the world. Kolkata also has the largest soccer stadium in India.

**Fact** Kolkata, formerly known as Calcutta, is the second-biggest city in India. It was the capital of British India and still boasts grand colonial architecture.

| City status | Regional capital |

City status
(see opposite page)

Page number

35

New York

4

# Factfile

**The vital statistics of a city are outlined in the Factfile. The Factfiles let you compare one city to another.**

**Population**
This indicates the total number of people who are permanently living within the city.

**Land area**
This entry is used to show the size of the city in terms of how much land it occupies. This measurement is shown in square miles.

**Density**
The is the average number of people living in a square mile of the city.

**Languages**
This indicates the languages that are used. An official language is one that is most widely spoken or used by government, education and business.

**Currency**
The name of the money that is used.

**Temperature**
This shows the highest and lowest average monthly temperatures recorded in the city.

**Top spot**
A brief description of an important place or cultural and historic site in or near the city.

**Fact**
The Fact panel highlights what has made or is making this city internationally important.

# City status

**Each city has a "City status." This describes the legal importance of the city within its region, state or country.**

**City**
These cities have no special status. They are defined as a city because of their population size.

**Regional capital**
This is the capital city of a political area of a country. The area may be a state, province, region or county.

**National capital**
This type of city is a seat of government and an administrative center of a country.

**Special administrative region**
These areas of the People's Republic of China have separate laws to those of the Republic.

**Legislative capital**
A city where the government has the power to make and change public policy.

**Federal city**
A city in a federal system is where some laws are made centrally, others are made more locally.

**City state**
A state that has its own government and consists of a city and the surrounding area.

5

# Rise of the megacity

As more and more of the world becomes urban, some cities are growing to phenomenal sizes. A megacity has a population of over 10 million and there are currently 30 megacities.

## Tokyo, Japan
### Population 37,843,000

Today, the larger metropolitan Tokyo area is home to more than 37 million people. It is the largest metropolitan area in the world by population. Tokyo has been divided into many smaller, often self-governing entities, including 23 "special wards" that form the core of this colossal megacity.

**Tokyo has some of the tallest buildings in the world**

## Seoul, South Korea
### Population 23,480,000

Seoul has boomed in just 50 years to become the world's 10th most economically powerful city and the world's second-largest metropolitan area. Nearly half of South Korea's population lives in the Seoul National Capital Area.

## Jakarta, Indonesia
### Population 30,539,000

Jakarta is the hub of Indonesia's economy, cultural life and politics. It can be divided into three sections: the old town with Javanese, Chinese and Arab quarters; central Jakarta with high-rise buildings; and the modern garden suburbs.

## Mexico City, Mexico
### Population 20,063,000

The population of Mexico City has grown by almost 20 million people in little more than a century, from 500,000 in 1900 to 20 million today. Mexico City is the richest city in Latin America, and the eighth richest in the world. It is a global city.

The sprawling South Korean city of Seoul lights up at night

# Contents

The towers of central Jakarta dwarf buildings in the old town

## Delhi, India
### Population 24,998,000
Delhi has been continuously inhabited since the 6th century. It is one of the fastest-growing cities in the world. Delhi is struggling to manage this rapid growth and is facing substantial pressure to improve its commercial and residential infrastructure. In addition, the city has to deal with dangerous levels of air pollution.

High-rise housing in Mexico City for the growing population

A view over the rooftops of Delhi from Jama Masjid mosque

# Gaborone

KHAMA III    SEBELE I    BATHOEN I

## Factfile

| | |
|---|---|
| **Population** | 422,000 |
| **Land area** | 85 square miles |
| **Density** | 5,000 people per square mile |
| **Languages** | Setswana and English (official) |
| **Currency** | Botswanan pula |
| **Temperature** | 86 °F (high) / 45 °F (low) |

**Top spot** The Three Dikgosi Monument is a bronze sculpture depicting three tribal chiefs who played important roles in Botswana's independence.

**Fact** Gaborone mixes city life with the wildlife of Botswana. The city has its own game reserve where you can see wildebeest, ostriches and warthogs.

**City status**          **National capital**

8

# Kinshasa

## Factfile

| | |
|---|---|
| **Population** | 11,587,000 |
| **Land area** | 225 square miles |
| **Density** | 51,500 people per square mile |
| **Languages** | French (official) and Lingala |
| **Currency** | Congolese franc |
| **Temperature** | 87 °F (high) / 70 °F (low) |

**Top spot** In the city's center is the Central Market with its famous food hall. Here the adventurous can try exotic foods, like snails, caterpillars and grasshoppers!

**Fact** Brazzaville (capital of the Republic of the Congo) and Kinshasa are the closest capital cities in the world. All that separates them is the Congo River.

| City status | National capital |
|---|---|

# Cairo

## Factfile

| | |
|---|---|
| **Population** | 15,600,000 |
| **Land area** | 680 square miles |
| **Density** | 22,900 people per square mile |
| **Language** | Arabic |
| **Currency** | Egyptian pound |
| **Temperature** | 93 °F (high) / 51 °F (low) |

**Top spot** The Museum of Egyptian Antiquities was opened in 1902. It contains over 120,000 of the world's most valuable ancient Egyptian artifacts.

**Fact** The longest river in the world flows through Cairo. The Nile is over 4,000 miles long and flows through 11 countries into the Mediterranean Sea.

| **City status** | **National capital** |
|---|---|

# Addis Ababa

## Factfile

| | |
|---|---|
| **Population** | 3,376,000 |
| **Land area** | 170 square miles |
| **Density** | 19,900 people per square mile |
| **Languages** | Amharic, Oromo, Tigrinya and Somali |
| **Currency** | Ethiopian birr |
| **Temperature** | 72 °F (high) / 51 °F (low) |

**Top spot** The National Museum houses a three-million-year-old fossilized human skeleton. Called "Lucy," she is one of the earliest ancestors of the human race.

**Fact** Addis Ababa means "new flower" in Amharic. This city, at an altitude of 7,726 feet above sea level, is the fifth-highest capital city in the world.

| City status | National capital |
|---|---|

11

# Accra

## Factfile

| | |
|---|---|
| **Population** | 4,145,000 |
| **Land area** | 375 square miles |
| **Density** | 11,100 people per square mile |
| **Languages** | English (official) and African languages |
| **Currency** | Ghanaian cedi |
| **Temperature** | 88 °F (high) / 74 °F (low) |

**Top spot** Independence Square, or Black Star Square, is the site of the Eternal Flame of African Liberation. It was lit in 1957 and is still burning to this day.

**Fact** Accra's economy centers on the manufacture of clothing, processed food and chemicals, and lumber, fishing, agriculture and finance.

**City status**      **National capital**

# Nairobi

## Factfile

| | |
|---|---|
| **Population** | 4,738,000 |
| **Land area** | 215 square miles |
| **Density** | 22,000 people per square mile |
| **Languages** | Kiswahili and English |
| **Currency** | Kenyan shilling |
| **Temperature** | 80 °F (high) / 54 °F (low) |

**Top spot** Nairobi National Park is located in the city – its skyscrapers can be seen through the reserve's fencing. It has a very successful rhinoceros sanctuary.

**Fact** Nairobi has a cooler temperature than many African cities. The original name for the city was "Ewaso Nai'beri," which means "place of cool waters."

| **City status** | **National capital** |
|---|---|

13

# Marrakech

## Factfile

| | |
|---|---|
| **Population** | 1,173,000 |
| **Land area** | 31 square miles |
| **Density** | 37,800 people per square mile |
| **Languages** | Arabic (official), Berber dialects and French |
| **Currency** | Moroccan dirham |
| **Temperature** | 97 °F (high) / 43 °F (low) |

**Top spot** Jemaa el Fna Square comes alive at night with people and entertainment. This square has been a meeting and trading place since the 11th century.

**Fact** The city of Marrakech was founded by the Almoravids, religious nomads who emerged from the south to build their capital on the Tensift River in 1062.

| City status | Regional capital |
|---|---|

# Lagos

## Factfile

| | |
|---|---|
| **Population** | 13,123,000 |
| **Land area** | 350 square miles |
| **Density** | 37,500 people per square mile |
| **Languages** | English (official), Hausa, Yoruba, Igbo and Fulani |
| **Currency** | Nigerian naira |
| **Temperature** | 86 °F (high) / 75 °F (low) |

**Top spot** Freedom Park is a cultural center and event venue. Located in an old prison, it celebrates Nigeria's independence in 1960 from British colonial rule.

**Fact** Lagos is Africa's second-busiest port. Though no longer the country's capital city, it has the highest population and is the most important financially.

| City status | City |
|---|---|

15

# Dakar

## Factfile

| | |
|---|---|
| **Population** | 3,520,000 |
| **Land area** | 75 square miles |
| **Density** | 46,900 people per square mile |
| **Languages** | French (official), Wolof, Pulaar and others |
| **Currency** | West African CFA franc |
| **Temperature** | 86 °F (high) / 64 °F (low) |

**Top spot** Intended as a symbol of Africa's future, The African Renaissance Monument has attracted much criticism. It is 1.5 times taller than the Statue of Liberty.

**Fact** Manufacturing industries in and around Dakar include peanut oil and petroleum refining, flour milling, fish canning and truck building.

| City status | National capital |
|---|---|

# Freetown

## Factfile

| | |
|---|---|
| **Population** | 1,000,000 |
| **Land area** | 35 square miles |
| **Density** | 28,600 people per square mile |
| **Languages** | Krio and English (official) |
| **Currency** | Sierra Leonean leone |
| **Temperature** | 80 °F (high) / 75 °F (low) |

**Top spot** Freetown's most famous landmark is a large cotton tree in the oldest part of town. Some believe the first settlers rested here when they first arrived.

**Fact** In 1787, a group of freed slaves from Great Britain settled in this part of Sierra Leone. Others joined them and the town was named Freetown.

| **City status** | **National capital** |
|---|---|

# Cape Town

## Factfile

| | |
|---|---|
| **Population** | 3,812,000 |
| **Land area** | 315 square miles |
| **Density** | 12,100 people per square mile |
| **Languages** | Zulu, Xhosa, Afrikaans, Sepedi, English, Setswana, Sesotho, Xitsonga and others |
| **Currency** | South African rand |
| **Temperature** | 78 °F (high) / 48 °F (low) |

**Top spot** From Cape Town you can trek to the top of Table Mountain, Devil's Peak, Lion's Head or Signal Hill for some amazing views across the bay.

**Fact** Cape Town was officially developed in 1652 by the Dutch East India Company. Prior to this the area was inhabited by the Khoisan people.

| **City status** | **Legislative capital** |
|---|---|

# Johannesburg

## Factfile

| | |
|---|---|
| **Population** | 8,432,000 |
| **Land area** | 1,000 square miles |
| **Density** | 8,400 people per square mile |
| **Languages** | Zulu, Xhosa, Afrikaans, Sepedi, English, Setswana, Sesotho, Xitsonga and others |
| **Currency** | South African rand |
| **Temperature** | 77 °F (high) / 41 °F (low) |

**Top spot** The Nelson Mandela Museum is dedicated to Mandela's memory and his struggle for freedom, democracy and change during South Africa's apartheid era.

**Fact** Johannesburg's nickname "eGoli" means "city of gold," which is a reference to its origin as a successful mining town in the late 19th century.

**City status**      **Regional capital**

# Tunis

## Factfile

| | |
|---|---|
| **Population** | 1,990,000 |
| **Land area** | 140 square miles |
| **Density** | 14,200 people per square mile |
| **Languages** | Arabic (official) and French |
| **Currency** | Tunisian dinar |
| **Temperature** | 90 °F (high) / 46 °F (low) |

**Top spot** The ruins of Carthage lie northeast of Tunis. Built 3,000 years ago by the Phoenicians, it was once one of the largest and busiest cities in the ancient world.

**Fact** From the 12th to the 16th century Tunis was one of the greatest and wealthiest cities of the Islamic world. Its history is reflected in its architecture.

| **City status** | **National capital** |
|---|---|

20

# Phnom Penh

## Factfile

| | |
|---|---|
| **Population** | 1,729,000 |
| **Land area** | 85 square miles |
| **Density** | 20,300 people per square mile |
| **Language** | Khmer |
| **Currency** | Cambodian riel |
| **Temperature** | 95 °F (high) / 69.8 °F (low) |

**Top spot** Central Market is an enormous yellow building that contains shops selling everything from antique coins, jewelry and flowers to fresh food.

**Fact** Phnom Penh, the "Pearl of Asia," is Cambodia's largest city. It is located at the intersection of the Mekong, Tonle Sap and Bassac rivers.

| City status | National capital |
|---|---|

# Beijing

## Factfile

| | |
|---|---|
| **Population** | 21,009,000 |
| **Land area** | 1,475 square miles |
| **Density** | 14,200 people per square mile |
| **Language** | Mandarin |
| **Currency** | Renminbi |
| **Temperature** | 86 °F (high) / 17 °F (low) |

**Top spot** The Forbidden City at the heart of Beijing was the imperial palace for 24 Ming and Qing emperors from 1416–1911. It is now a World Heritage Site.

**Fact** The name Beijing means "northern capital." It is believed that this area has been inhabited by modern humans for about 27,000 years.

| **City status** | **National capital** |
|---|---|

22

# Chengdu

## Factfile

| | |
|---|---|
| **Population** | 10,376,000 |
| **Land area** | 595 square miles |
| **Density** | 17,400 people per square mile |
| **Language** | Mandarin |
| **Currency** | Renminbi |
| **Temperature** | 84 °F (high) / 37 °F (low) |

**Top spot** Chengdu's most famous residents have a home all to themselves. Over 120 giant pandas live at the Giant Panda Breeding and Research Base.

**Fact** Paper money was first made and used in Chengdu in around 960. It was called Jiaozi, but the round coins with the square hole remained in use.

| **City status** | **Regional capital** |
|---|---|

# Dongguan

## Factfile

| | |
|---|---|
| **Population** | 8,442,000 |
| **Land area** | 625 square miles |
| **Density** | 13,500 people per square mile |
| **Language** | Mandarin |
| **Currency** | Renminbi |
| **Temperature** | 84 °F (high) / 57.6 °F (low) |

**Top spot** The Keyuan Garden contains traditional pavilions, bridges and ponds. With 130 doorways and 108 gateways, it is easy to get lost in this mazelike space.

**Fact** On the fifth day of the fifth month of the Chinese calendar, thousands flock to Dongguan for the noisy and colorful Dragon Boat Festival.

| City status | City |
|---|---|

# Guangzhou

## Factfile

| | |
|---|---|
| **Population** | 20,597,000 |
| **Land area** | 1,325 square miles |
| **Density** | 15,500 people per square mile |
| **Language** | Mandarin |
| **Currency** | Renminbi |
| **Temperature** | 90 °F (high) / 51 °F (low) |

**Top spot** The Temple of the Six Banyan Trees is an ancient but active Buddhist temple complex that was originally constructed nearly 1,500 years ago.

**Fact** Guangzhou is an important and historic port. It was the first Chinese port to begin trading with Europeans as far back as the 10th century.

| City status | Regional capital |
|---|---|

25

# Macau

## Factfile

| | |
|---|---|
| **Population** | 589,000 |
| **Land area** | 9 square miles |
| **Density** | 65,400 people per square mile |
| **Language** | Cantonese |
| **Currency** | Macanese pataca |
| **Temperature** | 90 °F (high) / 55 °F (low) |

**Top spot** Coloane, one of the oldest parts of Macau, has a swashbuckling past. Until the 1900s this area was used as a base by pirates sailing the South China Sea.

**Fact** Macau's population is 95 percent Chinese. The rest are people of mixed Portuguese-Chinese ancestry. Until 1999, Macau was a Portuguese territory.

| **City status** | **Special administrative region** |
|---|---|

# Shanghai

## Factfile

| | |
|---|---|
| **Population** | 23,416,000 |
| **Land area** | 1,475 square miles |
| **Density** | 15,900 people per square mile |
| **Language** | Mandarin |
| **Currency** | Renminbi |
| **Temperature** | 88 °F (high) / 34 °F (low) |

**Top spot** Oriental Pearl TV Tower is a 1,536-foot-high tower that dominates the skyline. It is the world's sixth- and China's second-tallest tower.

**Fact** Sitting at the mouth of Asia's longest river, the Yangtze, where it empties into the East China Sea, has made Shanghai the world's busiest shipping port.

| **City status** | **City** |
|---|---|

# Shenzhen

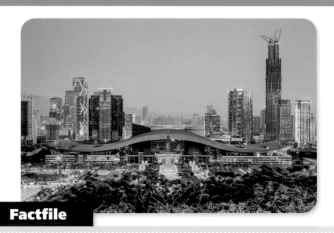

## Factfile

| | |
|---|---|
| **Population** | 12,084,000 |
| **Land area** | 675 square miles |
| **Density** | 17,900 people per square mile |
| **Language** | Mandarin |
| **Currency** | Renminbi |
| **Temperature** | 89 °F (high) / 50 °F (low) |

**Top spot** The Splendid China Folk Village is a large theme park built to teach visitors all about China's ethnic groups, famous sites and architectural heritage.

**Fact** Shenzhen was a market town until it became China's first Special Economic Zone in 1980. Today, it is a financial center and China's "Silicon Valley."

| City status | City |
|---|---|

28

# Tianjin

## Factfile

| | |
|---|---|
| **Population** | 10,920,000 |
| **Land area** | 775 square miles |
| **Density** | 14,100 people per square mile |
| **Language** | Mandarin |
| **Currency** | Renminbi |
| **Temperature** | 86 °F (high) / 20 °F (low) |

**Top spot** Tianjin has many historic buildings and markets. The Huangya Pass, a section of the Great Wall of China, is located a few miles outside of the city.

**Fact** In the 19th century Western nations used Tianjin as a port and as access to Beijing. Today, it is Beijing's gateway to the West and an economic powerhouse.

| **City status** | **City** |
|---|---|

# Hong Kong

## Factfile

| | |
|---|---|
| **Population** | 7,246,000 |
| **Land area** | 106 square miles |
| **Density** | 68,400 people per square mile |
| **Languages** | Cantonese and English |
| **Currency** | Hong Kong dollar |
| **Temperature** | 87.8 °F (high) / 57.2 °F (low) |

**Top spot** Victoria Peak, which can be reached by an historic funicular railway, is a mountain on Hong Kong Island and offers views across the harbor and city.

**Fact** Hong Kong is ranked as the world's leading trade and financial center. It is densely populated and has more skyscrapers than any other city, even New York!

| City status | Special administrative region |
|---|---|

# Agra

## Factfile

| | |
|---|---|
| **Population** | 1,938,000 |
| **Land area** | 50 square miles |
| **Density** | 38,800 people per square mile |
| **Languages** | Hindi and 14 other official languages and English |
| **Currency** | Indian rupee |
| **Temperature** | 107.1 °F (high) / 45.9 °F (low) |

**Top spot** The Taj Mahal is known as a symbol of love. The Mughal emperor, Shah Jahan, built the mausoleum to house the remains of his beloved wife.

**Fact** As Agra is home to three World Heritage Sites – the Taj Mahal, Red Fort and Fatehpur Sikri – tourism has become the mainstay of the city's economy.

| **City status** | **City** |
|---|---|

# Bengaluru

## Factfile

| | |
|---|---|
| **Population** | 9,807,000 |
| **Land area** | 450 square miles |
| **Density** | 21,800 people per square mile |
| **Languages** | Kannad (official), English, Telugu, Tamil and Hindi |
| **Currency** | Indian rupee |
| **Temperature** | 93 °F (high) / 59 °F (low) |

**Top spot** The Krishna Rajendra Market is filled with foods, spices, dyes, textiles and copperware. There is a colorful flower market hidden at the market's center.

**Fact** Bengaluru (formerly Bangalore) is the capital of the Indian state of Karnataka. The city is home to hundreds of IT firms and educational institutions.

**City status** | **Regional capital**

# Chennai

## Factfile

| | |
|---|---|
| **Population** | 9,714,000 |
| **Land area** | 375 square miles |
| **Density** | 25,900 people per square mile |
| **Languages** | Tamil and English (official), Telugu and Hindi |
| **Currency** | Indian rupee |
| **Temperature** | 99.3 °F (high) / 68.7 °F (low) |

**Top spot** The Kapaleeswarar Temple is believed to be one of the oldest and holiest places in the city. This shrine to Shiva hosts a 10-day festival each year.

**Fact** Chennai's growing economy is due to its chemical, automotive, software, hardware and textile industries. This city is known as the "Detroit of India."

| City status | Regional capital |
|---|---|

# Hyderabad

## Factfile

| | |
|---|---|
| **Population** | 8,754,000 |
| **Land area** | 475 square miles |
| **Density** | 18,400 people per square mile |
| **Languages** | Telugu (official), Urdu, Hindi and English |
| **Currency** | Indian rupee |
| **Temperature** | 102.2 °F (high) / 58 °F (low) |

**Top spot** The Ramoji Film City is the largest film studio in the world. It creates films in multiple languages for Telugu, Tamil and Hindi speakers.

**Fact** Hyderabad was historically a pearl and diamond trading center, but today it is known for its pharmaceutical and biotechnology companies.

| City status | Regional capital |
|---|---|

# Kolkata

## Factfile

| | |
|---|---|
| **Population** | 14,667,000 |
| **Land area** | 465 square miles |
| **Density** | 31,500 people per square mile |
| **Languages** | Bengali, English and Urdu (official) and Hindi |
| **Currency** | Indian rupee |
| **Temperature** | 96.7 °F (high) / 57.6 °F (low) |

**Top spot** The Calcutta Football League, started in 1898, is one of the oldest leagues in the world. Kolkata also has the largest soccer stadium in India.

**Fact** Kolkata, formerly known as Calcutta, is the second-biggest city in India. It was the capital of British India and still boasts grand colonial architecture.

| City status | Regional capital |
|---|---|

35

# Mumbai

## Factfile

| | |
|---|---|
| **Population** | 17,712,000 |
| **Land area** | 211 square miles |
| **Density** | 83,900 people per square mile |
| **Languages** | Marathi (official), Hindi and English |
| **Currency** | Indian rupee |
| **Temperature** | 92.3 °F (high) / 62.1 °F (low) |

**Top spot** The Sanjay Gandhi National Park is a Mumbai oasis. Its forest has panthers, among other animals, and ancient hand-carved Buddhist caves.

**Fact** By 2020, Mumbai's population may reach 28 million, making it the world's most populous city. This noisy, bustling city is also the hub of India's film industry.

| City status | Regional capital |
|---|---|

# New Delhi

## Factfile

| | |
|---|---|
| **Population** | 11,008,000 |
| **Land area** | 800 square miles |
| **Density** | 31,200 people per square mile |
| **Languages** | Hindi (official), English, Urdu and Punjabi |
| **Currency** | Indian rupee |
| **Temperature** | 104 °F (high) / 44 °F (low) |

**Top spot** The Baha'i Lotus Temple was opened to the public in 1986. Built in the shape of a lotus flower it symbolizes love, peace, purity and immortality.

**Fact** New Delhi, one of 11 districts in Delhi, is a cosmopolitan city and the country's administrative center. Much of the British architecture remains in use.

**City status**      **National capital**

# Jakarta

## Factfile

| | |
|---|---|
| **Population** | 30,539,000 |
| **Land area** | 1,245 square miles |
| **Density** | 24,500 people per square mile |
| **Languages** | Indonesian (official), English, Dutch and dialects |
| **Currency** | Indonesian rupiah |
| **Temperature** | 89 °F (high) / 74 °F (low) |

**Top spot** The Monas is a 433-foot-tall tower in Merdeka Square. This national monument represents the struggle of the Indonesian people to achieve freedom.

**Fact** Jakarta has had many names since it was founded over 1,000 years ago. It has been called Sunda Kelapa, Jayakarta, Batavia and Djakarta.

| **City status** | **National capital** |
|---|---|

# Baghdad

## Factfile

| | |
|---|---|
| **Population** | 6,625,000 |
| **Land area** | 260 square miles |
| **Density** | 25,500 people per square mile |
| **Languages** | Arabic and Kurdish |
| **Currency** | Iraqi dinar |
| **Temperature** | 108 °F (high) / 38 °F (low) |

**Top spot** The Al-Kadhimiya Mosque is considered a very holy place. It contains the tombs of several historical scholars and spiritual and political leaders.

**Fact** Baghdad is the largest city in Iraq and is situated on both sides of the Tigris River. The city was originally founded in the 8th century.

| **City status** | **National capital** |
|---|---|

# Tehran

## Factfile

| | |
|---|---|
| **Population** | 13,532,000 |
| **Land area** | 575 square miles |
| **Density** | 23,500 people per square mile |
| **Language** | Persian |
| **Currency** | Iranian rial |
| **Temperature** | 97 °F (high) / 29 °F (low) |

**Top spot** Tehran's Grand Bazaar is a six-mile maze of bustling alleys. Traders have been hawking their wares on this site for nearly 1,000 years.

**Fact** Tehran is the largest city and the economic center of Iran. Industries in the city include automotive, electronics, textiles, sugar and cement.

| **City status** | **National capital** |
|---|---|

# Jerusalem

## Factfile

| | |
|---|---|
| **Population** | 840,000 |
| **Land area** | 90 square miles |
| **Density** | 9,300 people per square mile |
| **Languages** | Hebrew (official), Arabic and English |
| **Currency** | New Israeli shekel |
| **Temperature** | 85 °F (high) / 43.5 °F (low) |

**Top spot** Al-Aqsa is the biggest mosque in Jerusalem and the third-holiest site in Islam. It is large enough for 4,000 Muslims to pray together during worship.

**Fact** Jerusalem is one of the oldest cities in the world, with parts of the city dating from 4000 BCE. It is a holy city for Jews, Christians and Muslims.

| **City status** | **National capital** |
|---|---|

41

# Nagoya

## Factfile

| | |
|---|---|
| **Population** | 10,177,000 |
| **Land area** | 1,500 square miles |
| **Density** | 6,800 people per square mile |
| **Language** | Japanese |
| **Currency** | Japanese yen |
| **Temperature** | 89 °F (high) / 31 °F (low) |

**Top spot** One of Japan's most revered Shinto shrines – the Atsuta Shrine – is in Nagoya. Established in the 1st century, over nine million people visit it each year.

**Fact** Nagoya is a shipping hub with a history of manufacturing machines, large and small. Many car and automotive industries are based here.

| **City status** | **Regional capital** |
|---|---|

# Osaka

## Factfile

| | |
|---|---|
| **Population** | 17,444,000 |
| **Land area** | 1,240 square miles |
| **Density** | 14,100 people per square mile |
| **Language** | Japanese |
| **Currency** | Japanese yen |
| **Temperature** | 91 °F (high) / 33 °F (low) |

**Top spot** Shitenno-ji is Japan's first and oldest Buddhist temple. Constructed over 1,400 years ago by Prince Shotoku, it has been rebuilt many times.

**Fact** Osaka's – the nation's kitchen – was the historical center for the rice trade. This merchant class created the city's current commercial prominence.

| **City status** | **Regional capital** |
|---|---|

# Tokyo

## Factfile

| | |
|---|---|
| **Population** | 37,843,000 |
| **Land area** | 3,300 square miles |
| **Density** | 11,500 people per square mile |
| **Language** | Japanese |
| **Currency** | Japanese yen |
| **Temperature** | 86 °F (high) / 35 °F (low) |

**Top spot** The Tokyo Tower, built in 1958, was modeled on Paris's Eiffel Tower, but it is taller. It is the tallest self-supporting steel structure in the world!

**Fact** Tokyo was previously known as Edo. Edo grew from a tiny fishing village of the 15th century to the largest city in the world by the 18th century.

**City status**      **National capital**

# Kuala Lumpur

## Factfile

| | |
|---|---|
| **Population** | 7,088,000 |
| **Land area** | 750 square miles |
| **Density** | 9,500 people per square mile |
| **Languages** | Malay (official), English, Chinese dialects and Tamil |
| **Currency** | Malaysian ringgit |
| **Temperature** | 91 °F (high) / 73 °F (low) |

**Top spot** During the Hindu festival of Thaipusam, many worshippers and tourists climb the 272 steps to the temples and shrines in the Batu Caves.

**Fact** Kuala Lumpur began life in 1857 when the area opened for tin mining. The first miners were Chinese, which is why it has a high Chinese population.

| **City status** | **National capital** |
|---|---|

# Karachi

## Factfile

**Population**     22,123,000
**Land area**      365 square miles
**Density**        60,600 people per square mile
**Languages**      Urdu and English (official), Punjabi and Sindhi
**Currency**       Pakistani rupee
**Temperature**    91 °F (high) / 55 °F (low)

**Top spot**  The marble structure of Mazar-e-Quaid is also known as the National Mausoleum. It is the tomb of the founder of Pakistan and was built in 1970.

**Fact**  Ancient Greeks called it Krokola, fisherman named it Kolachi, but this largest city in the Muslim world is now the "City of Light" for it never sleeps.

| City status | Reginal capital |
|---|---|

46

# Lahore

## Factfile

| | |
|---|---|
| **Population** | 10,052,000 |
| **Land area** | 305 square miles |
| **Density** | 33,000 people per square mile |
| **Languages** | Urdu (official), English and Punjabi |
| **Currency** | Pakistani rupee |
| **Temperature** | 102 °F (high) / 48 °F (low) |

**Top spot** Badshahi is the seventh-largest mosque in the world. It can accommodate 10,000 faithful in the prayer hall and 100,000 in the courtyard.

**Fact** The city of Lahore is the capital of the Pakistani province of Punjab. It occupies a central position, and is generally called "The Heart of Pakistan."

**City status**      **Reginal capital**

47

# Manila

## Factfile

| | |
|---|---|
| **Population** | 24,123,000 |
| **Land area** | 610 square miles |
| **Density** | 39,500 people per square mile |
| **Languages** | Filipino and English |
| **Currency** | Philippine peso |
| **Temperature** | 93 °F (high) / 71 °F (low) |

**Top spot** Quiapo Church is home to the shrine of the Black Nazarene, a statue of Jesus Christ carved by an anonymous Mexican artist in black wood.

**Fact** Built on geological fault lines and across a typhoon belt, this highly populous city has been ranked as the second-most dangerous in which to live.

**City status**      **National capital**

# Mecca

## Factfile

| | |
|---|---|
| **Population** | 1,647,000 |
| **Land area** | 150 square miles |
| **Density** | 11,000 people per square mile |
| **Language** | Arabic |
| **Currency** | Saudi riyal |
| **Temperature** | 109 °F (high) / 65 °F (low) |

**Top spot** Every year around two million Muslims travel to Mecca for the hajj, a pilgrimage to Islam's holiest shrine, the Kaaba (the Cube), at the Sacred Mosque.

**Fact** Mecca, as the birthplace of Muhammad and where the Koran was revealed, is the holiest city in the religion of Islam.

| **City status** | **Regional capital** |
|---|---|

49

# Riyadh

## Factfile

| | |
|---|---|
| **Population** | 5,666,000 |
| **Land area** | 580 square miles |
| **Density** | 9,800 people per square mile |
| **Language** | Arabic |
| **Currency** | Saudi riyal |
| **Temperature** | 109 °F (high) / 48 °F (low) |

**Top spot** The Kingdom Center – a 99-story tower with a sky bridge joining the two sides – is a prominent landmark and attraction in Riyadh.

**Fact** Built on a desert trading route, Riyadh is one of the wealthiest cities in the world. Much of this wealth has come from its oil reserves.

| City status | National capital |
|---|---|

# Singapore

## Factfile

| | |
|---|---|
| **Population** | 5,624,000 |
| **Land area** | 200 square miles |
| **Density** | 28,100 people per square mile |
| **Languages** | English, Malay, Mandarin and Tamil |
| **Currency** | Singapore dollar |
| **Temperature** | 89 °F (high) / 75 °F (low) |

**Top spot** Raffles Hotel, a world famous hotel, opened in 1887. It was made a national monument and many famous people have stayed at this colonial institution.

**Fact** Singapore is one of a few countries in the world that is an island, a city and a state at the same time! Singapore, from the Malay, means "lion city."

| City status | City state |
|---|---|

## Factfile

| | |
|---|---|
| **Population** | 23,480,000 |
| **Land area** | 875 square miles |
| **Density** | 26,800 people per square mile |
| **Languages** | Gyeonggi |
| **Currency** | South Korean won |
| **Temperature** | 84 °F (high) / 21 °F (low) |

**Top spot** Gyeongbokgung, a grand palace, was razed in the 1590s and left in ruins for 273 years. Rebuilt in 1867, its 500 buildings form a small city.

**Fact** Seoul is a highly modern city where technology industries have replaced the traditional industries of textiles and clothing manufacture.

| City status | National capital |

# Taipei

## Factfile

| | |
|---|---|
| **Population** | 7,438,000 |
| **Land area** | 440 square miles |
| **Density** | 16,900 people per square mile |
| **Languages** | Mandarin (official), Taiwanese and Hakka |
| **Currency** | New Taiwan dollar |
| **Temperature** | 92 °F (high) / 55 °F (low) |

**Top spot** At 1,667 feet, Taipei 101 Tower is the world's tallest eco building. Designed to resemble a bamboo plant, it is typhoon and earthquake resistant.

**Fact** Taipei and its surrounding areas are significant industrial areas of Taiwan. It has become a top producer of computer technology and components.

| **City status** | **National capital** |
|---|---|

# Bankgok

## Factfile

| | |
|---|---|
| **Population** | 14,998,000 |
| **Land area** | 1,000 square miles |
| **Density** | 15,000 people per square mile |
| **Language** | Thai |
| **Currency** | Thai baht |
| **Temperature** | 94 °F (high) / 70 °F (low) |

**Top spot** The city's spiritual heart is the Grand Palace. Built in 1782, it includes beautiful temples – one housing the Emerald Buddha – halls and gardens.

**Fact** Bangkok was once nicknamed "Venice of the East" as dozens of canals crisscrossed the city and buildings stood on stilts. Most canals have now been filled in.

| **City status** | **National capital** |
|---|---|

54

# Ankara

## Factfile

| | |
|---|---|
| **Population** | 4,538,000 |
| **Land area** | 255 square miles |
| **Density** | 17,800 people per square mile |
| **Languages** | Turkish (official), Kurdish and Arabic |
| **Currency** | Turkish lira |
| **Temperature** | 83.0 °F (high) / 20.0 °F (low) |

**Top spot** Ankara Castle sits on an outcrop and it has 42 five-sided towers along its walls. The inner area of the fortress is still inhabited by local people.

**Fact** Ankara became the capital in 1923 when the republic was founded after the fall of the Ottoman Empire that had its capital in Istanbul.

| **City status** | **National capital** |
|---|---|

# Dubai

## Factfile

| | |
|---|---|
| **Population** | 3,933,000 |
| **Land area** | 520 square miles |
| **Density** | 7,600 people per square mile |
| **Languages** | Arabic (official), English, Persian, Hindi and Urdu |
| **Currency** | United Arab Emirates dirham |
| **Temperature** | 103 °F (high) / 58 °F (low) |

**Top spot** The Burj al Arab, which stands on an artificial island, has been called the world's only seven-star hotel. Sail shaped, it has a helipad at roof height.

**Fact** Everything about Dubai is record breaking. It has the world's tallest building, the world's fastest roller coaster and an indoor ski resort!

| City status | City |
|---|---|

56

# Hanoi

## Factfile

| | |
|---|---|
| **Population** | 3,715,000 |
| **Land area** | 180 square miles |
| **Density** | 20,600 people per square mile |
| **Language** | Vietnamese |
| **Currency** | Vietnamese dong |
| **Temperature** | 90 °F (high) / 59 °F (low) |

**Top spot** Long Bien Bridge across the Red River is 1.5 miles long. The defense of this vital bridge in the Vietnam War is recalled in song and poetry in Hanoi.

**Fact** In 2010, Hanoi marked 1,000 years of being a city. Once a French colony, markets and temples sit alongside shiny towers and industrial parks.

| **City status** | **National capital** |
|---|---|

# Ho Chi Minh City

## Factfile

| | |
|---|---|
| **Population** | 8,957,000 |
| **Land area** | 575 square miles |
| **Density** | 15,600 people per square mile |
| **Language** | Vietnamese |
| **Currency** | Vietnamese dong |
| **Temperature** | 93 °F (high) / 72 °F (low) |

**Top spot** The Saigon Notre Dame Cathedral was built between 1863 and 1880 by the French colonists. It is considered an iconic symbol of the city.

**Fact** Previously called Saigon and the nation's capital, H.C.M.C. is Vietnam's largest city. Its industries include mining, agriculture and trade.

| City status | City |
|---|---|

58

# Melbourne

## Factfile

| | |
|---|---|
| **Population** | 3,906,000 |
| **Land area** | 982 square miles |
| **Density** | 3,800 people per square mile |
| **Language** | English |
| **Currency** | Australian dollar |
| **Temperature** | 80 °F (high) / 41 °F (low) |

**Top spot** Melbourne Museum is the largest museum in the southern hemisphere and is near the World Heritage-listed Royal Exhibition Building.

**Fact** Melbourne, situated on Port Phillip, was transformed from struggling settlement to large, wealthy city during the gold rushes of the 1850s.

| **City status** | **Regional capital** |
|---|---|

# Sydney

## Factfile

| | |
|---|---|
| **Population** | 4,036,000 |
| **Land area** | 786 square miles |
| **Density** | 5,000 people per square mile |
| **Language** | English |
| **Currency** | Australian dollar |
| **Temperature** | 79 °F (high) / 44 °F (low) |

**Top spot** Sydney Opera House is a performing arts center. Sitting on the harbor, its roofs resembling shells or sails, it is an iconic building that opened in 1973.

**Fact** Built on the world's largest natural harbor, Sydney went from 19th-century penal colony to leading financial center and tourist hot spot.

| City status | Regional capital |
|---|---|

# Honolulu

## Factfile

| | |
|---|---|
| **Population** | 842,000 |
| **Land area** | 170 square miles |
| **Density** | 4,700 people per square mile |
| **Languages** | Hawaiian and English |
| **Currency** | United States dollar |
| **Temperature** | 88.6 °F (high) / 66.1 °F (low) |

**Top spot** Iolani Palace is the only royal palace in the US. Built in 1882, it was lived in for only a few years before the monarchy was overthrown in 1893.

**Fact** Honolulu is the capital of Hawaii and is one of the most racially diversified cities in the US. Alongside tourism, it is a Pacific trading hub.

**City status**      **Regional capital**

# Wellington

## Factfile

| | |
|---|---|
| **Population** | 370,000 |
| **Land area** | 71 square miles |
| **Density** | 5,200 people per square mile |
| **Language** | English |
| **Currency** | New Zealand dollar |
| **Temperature** | 69.1 °F (high) / 43.3 °F (low) |

**Top spot**
The Wellington Cable Car, established in 1902, travels 0.4 miles uphill from Lambton Quay to the Botanic Gardens and the Carter Observatory.

**Fact**
Wellington is New Zealand's center of government and the world's southernmost capital city. Almost all residents live within two miles of the ocean.

| City status | National capital |
|---|---|

62

# Vienna

## Factfile

| | |
|---|---|
| **Population** | 1,763,000 |
| **Land area** | 175 square miles |
| **Density** | 10,100 people per square mile |
| **Language** | German |
| **Currency** | Euro |
| **Temperature** | 80.1 °F (high) / 30.6 °F (low) |

**Top spot** Schonbrunn Palace includes the mansion, a park and Vienna Zoo. The 1,441-room Baroque palace was declared a World Cultural Heritage Site in 1996.

**Fact** Vienna has been famous for its music for centuries. Mozart and Beethoven worked in Vienna, while Strauss I and II and Schubert were born here.

| **City status** | **National capital** |
|---|---|

# Brussels

## Factfile

| | |
|---|---|
| **Population** | 2,089,000 |
| **Land area** | 310 square miles |
| **Density** | 6,700 people per square mile |
| **Languages** | Dutch, French and German |
| **Currency** | Euro |
| **Temperature** | 72 °F (high) / 33 °F (low) |

**Top spot** The Atomium is an unusual monument made of nine metal spheres. It was made in 1958 to symbolize science and the arrival of the atomic age.

**Fact** Brussels is not only the capital of Belgium, but is also the home of the European Union, an economic and political union of 28 countries.

| City status | National capital |
|---|---|

64

# Sofia

## Factfile

| | |
|---|---|
| **Population** | 1,195,000 |
| **Land area** | 80 square miles |
| **Density** | 14,900 people per square mile |
| **Language** | Bulgarian |
| **Currency** | Bulgarian lev |
| **Temperature** | 78 °F (high) / 25 °F (low) |

**Top spot** The golden dome of St. Alexander Nevsky Cathedral defines the Sofia skyline. This beautiful cathedral can accommodate over 10,000 worshippers.

**Fact** Sofia has a long history spanning nearly 7,000 years, making it Europe's second-oldest city. Its motto is: "Grows, but does not age."

| City status | National capital |
|---|---|

65

# Zagreb

## Factfile

| | |
|---|---|
| **Population** | 704,000 |
| **Land area** | 72 square miles |
| **Density** | 9,800 people per square mile |
| **Language** | Croatian |
| **Currency** | Croatian kuna |
| **Temperature** | 81 °F (high) / 27 °F (low) |

**Top spot** The Mimara Museum is the city's crown jewel. It is named after a private collector who generously left thousands of priceless objects to the city.

**Fact** Croatia declared independence from Yugoslavia in 1991, and Zagreb became its capital. Nearly a quarter of all Croatians live in this city.

| City status | National capital |
|---|---|

# Prague

## Factfile

| | |
|---|---|
| **Population** | 1,310,000 |
| **Land area** | 110 square miles |
| **Density** | 11,900 people per square mile |
| **Language** | Czech |
| **Currency** | Czech crown |
| **Temperature** | 73 °F (high) / 24 °F (low) |

**Top spot** At the heart of the city is the 9th-century Prague Castle. It is the largest medieval castle in Europe, covering an area of seven soccer fields.

**Fact** Prague is the best-preserved medieval city in Europe and its nickname is "City of a Hundred Spires." Its historic center is a World Heritage Site.

| **City status** | **National capital** |
|---|---|

# Copenhagen

## Factfile

| | |
|---|---|
| **Population** | 1,248,000 |
| **Land area** | 175 square miles |
| **Density** | 6,700 people per square mile |
| **Language** | Danish |
| **Currency** | Danish krone |
| **Temperature** | 69 °F (high) / 28 °F (low) |

**Top spot** The Tivoli Gardens is a 150-year-old amusement park, still open today. Famous visitors include Hans Christian Andersen and Walt Disney.

**Fact** Copenhagen has been the winner of the world's happiest city, most eco-friendly capital and most livable city. It is also a top 20 tourist destination.

**City status**      **National capital**

# Tallinn

## Factfile

| | |
|---|---|
| **Population** | 380,000 |
| **Land area** | 70 square miles |
| **Density** | 5,400 people per square mile |
| **Languages** | Estonian (official) and Russian |
| **Currency** | Euro |
| **Temperature** | 70.2 °F (high) / 18.5 °F (low) |

**Top spot** The Old Town, built between the 13th and 16th centuries, has colorful houses and hidden courtyards surrounded by an ancient stone city wall.

**Fact** Built in a naturally formed harbor on the Baltic Sea, Tallinn is a city that mixes its medieval history with a modern, vibrant business and arts community.

| City status | National capital |
|---|---|

# Helsinki

## Factfile

| | |
|---|---|
| **Population** | 1,208,000 |
| **Land area** | 247 square miles |
| **Density** | 4,800 people per square mile |
| **Languages** | Finnish and Swedish |
| **Currency** | Euro |
| **Temperature** | 70 °F (high) / 20 °F (low) |

**Top spot** Situated on six islands off Helsinki is one of the world's largest sea fortresses. Suomenlinna (Castle of Finland) was made a World Heritage Site in 1991.

**Fact** Helsinki lies on the southern coast of Finland. The city is spread across the many islands in the bay. There are around 330 islands in Helsinki!

| City status | National capital |
|---|---|

# Paris

## Factfile

| | |
|---|---|
| **Population** | 10,858,000 |
| **Land area** | 1,098 square miles |
| **Density** | 9,500 people per square mile |
| **Language** | French |
| **Currency** | Euro |
| **Temperature** | 77.4 °F (high) / 36.9 °F (low) |

**Top spot** Built in 1889, the Eiffel Tower is the most famous symbol of Paris. For over 40 years it was the tallest man-made structure in the world.

**Fact** Paris is known for its rich cultural life and culinary traditions. Many of the world's most revered writers, artists and thinkers lived here.

| **City status** | **National capital** |
|---|---|

# Berlin

## Factfile

| | |
|---|---|
| **Population** | 4,069,000 |
| **Land area** | 520 square miles |
| **Density** | 7,800 people per square mile |
| **Language** | German |
| **Currency** | Euro |
| **Temperature** | 73 °F (high) / 30 °F (low) |

**Top spot** The Brandenburg Gate is the city's most iconic landmark. It became a symbol of unity and peace when the Berlin Wall was torn down in 1990.

**Fact** Berlin is crisscrossed by five rivers and six canals, creating 60 miles of navigable waterways. The city has about 900 bridges, which is more than Venice!

| City status | National capital |
|---|---|

# Athens

## Factfile

| | |
|---|---|
| **Population** | 3,484,000 |
| **Land area** | 225 square miles |
| **Density** | 15,500 people per square mile |
| **Language** | Greek |
| **Currency** | Euro |
| **Temperature** | 89.2 °F (high) / 44.6 °F (low) |

**Top spot** The Acropolis is a complex of ancient buildings high above the city. The Parthenon, built in 447 BCE, is one of the temples on the Acropolis.

**Fact** Athens is considered the birthplace of democracy, Western philosophy and literature, the Olympic Games, political science and theater.

| **City status** | **National capital** |
|---|---|

# Budapest

## Factfile

| | |
|---|---|
| **Population** | 1,710,000 |
| **Land area** | 345 square miles |
| **Density** | 5,000 people per square mile |
| **Language** | Hungarian |
| **Currency** | Hungarian forint |
| **Temperature** | 79 °F (high) / 25 °F (low) |

**Top spot** Built in 1902, the Hungarian Parliament is the world's third-largest legislative building. It is 315 feet high and has 691 rooms and 12.5 miles of stairs!

**Fact** Budapest is divided by the Danube River, and is actually two cities. Buda lies on the hilly west bank, and Pest is on the sandy plain to the east.

| City status | National capital |
|---|---|

# Reykjavik

## Factfile

| | |
|---|---|
| **Population** | 185,000 |
| **Land area** | 31 square miles |
| **Density** | 6,000 people per square mile |
| **Language** | Icelandic |
| **Currency** | Icelandic krona |
| **Temperature** | 55 °F (high) / 27 °F (low) |

**Top spot** The Lutheran Church of Hallgrimur is the city's most striking landmark. Its design echoes the landscape of volcanoes, ice caps and basalt columns.

**Fact** Reykjavik translates to "smoke cove" and is a reference to the hot springs and geysers in the area. It is the world's most-northern capital city.

| City status | National capital |
|---|---|

75

# Dublin

## Factfile

| | |
|---|---|
| **Population** | 1,160,000 |
| **Land area** | 175 square miles |
| **Density** | 6,600 people per square mile |
| **Languages** | English and Irish |
| **Currency** | Euro |
| **Temperature** | 67.1 °F (high) / 36.1 °F (low) |

**Top spot** Dublin's university, Trinity College, was created by Elizabeth I and has many well-respected graduates, including Bram Stoker, author of "Dracula."

**Fact** Dublin is on Ireland's east coast and is built on the River Liffey. One of its oldest industries is brewing, with Guinness possibly its most famous.

| City status | National capital |
|---|---|

# Rome

## Factfile

| | |
|---|---|
| **Population** | 3,906,000 |
| **Land area** | 430 square miles |
| **Density** | 9,100 people per square mile |
| **Language** | Italian |
| **Currency** | Euro |
| **Temperature** | 83.7 °F (high) / 38.7 °F (low) |

**Top spot** The Colosseum is an ancient amphitheater where a variety of events such as gladiator contests, mock battles and hunts, and dramas took place.

**Fact** Rome is famous for being the center of the Roman Empire, an ancient civilization that controlled Northern Africa, Europe and Great Britain.

| City status | National capital |
|---|---|

# Venice

## Factfile

| | |
|---|---|
| **Population** | 426,000 |
| **Land area** | 50 square miles |
| **Density** | 8,500 people per square mile |
| **Language** | Italian |
| **Currency** | Euro |
| **Temperature** | 81.5 °F (high) / 30.4 °F (low) |

**Top spot** St. Mark's Basilica is a magnificent cathedral in Venice. Its interior is decorated with 85,000 square feet of mosaics, most dating from the 12th century.

**Fact** Built on 118 islands in a lagoon, it has 170 canals and about 400 bridges. Once a maritime power, it is now a destination for 20 million tourists a year.

| City status | Regional capital |
|---|---|

# Amsterdam

## Factfile

| | |
|---|---|
| **Population** | 1,624,000 |
| **Land area** | 195 square miles |
| **Density** | 8,300 people per square mile |
| **Language** | Dutch |
| **Currency** | Euro |
| **Temperature** | 70 °F (high) / 32 °F (low) |

**Top spot** Rijksmuseum is the national art museum where masterpieces by great Dutch artists like Rembrandt, Johannes Vermeer and Frans Hals are shown.

**Fact** Amsterdam, founded over 770 years ago, is the most watery city in the world! A quarter of of the city's area consists of canals and harbors.

| City status | National capital |
|---|---|

# Oslo

## Factfile

| | |
|---|---|
| **Population** | 975,000 |
| **Land area** | 112 square miles |
| **Density** | 8,300 people per square mile |
| **Language** | Norwegian |
| **Currency** | Norwegian krone |
| **Temperature** | 71 °F (high) / 19 °F (low) |

**Top spot** The ceremony for the Nobel Peace Prize, which honors a person who has worked for unity and peace, is held each December in Oslo's City Hall.

**Fact** Oslo has been Norway's capital since 1814 when the country gained independence from Denmark. It is one of Europe's fastest-growing cities.

**City status**          **National capital**

# Warsaw

## Factfile

| | |
|---|---|
| **Population** | 1,720,000 |
| **Land area** | 210 square miles |
| **Density** | 8,200 people per square mile |
| **Language** | Polish |
| **Currency** | Polish zloty |
| **Temperature** | 73 °F (high) / 24 °F (low) |

**Top spot** Warsaw's tallest building, the Palace of Culture and Science, was a gift from Soviet Russia in 1945 to the country that it then controlled.

**Fact** Warsaw is known as the "Phoenix City" as it had to be rebuilt after 85 percent of its buildings were destroyed during World War Two.

| City status | National capital |
|---|---|

81

# Lisbon

## Factfile

| | |
|---|---|
| **Population** | 2,666,000 |
| **Land area** | 370 square miles |
| **Density** | 7,200 people per square mile |
| **Language** | Portuguese |
| **Currency** | Euro |
| **Temperature** | 82 °F (high) / 46.6 °F (low) |

**Top spot** Belem Tower is a symbol of the city. Built in the 1500s, this 100-foot stone watchtower and ceremonial gateway is a World Heritage Site.

**Fact** Lisbon is the second-oldest European capital after Athens. Many historians believe that the Phoenicians had a trading post here in 1200 BCE.

| City status | National capital |
|---|---|

# Bucharest

## Factfile

| | |
|---|---|
| **Population** | 1,860,000 |
| **Land area** | 110 square miles |
| **Density** | 16,900 people per square mile |
| **Language** | Romanian |
| **Currency** | Romanian leu |
| **Temperature** | 82 °F (high) / 23 °F (low) |

**Top spot** Initially built of wood in 1922 to honor the bravery of Romanian soldiers, Bucharest's 85-foot-high Arch of Triumph was finished in granite in 1936.

**Fact** Bucharest has often been called "Little Paris" because of its beautiful boulevards, elegant architecture, luxurious hotels and exotic restaurants.

| **City status** | **National capital** |
|---|---|

# Belgrade

## Factfile

| | |
|---|---|
| **Population** | 1,180,000 |
| **Land area** | 90 square miles |
| **Density** | 13,100 people per square mile |
| **Language** | Serbian |
| **Currency** | Serbian dinar |
| **Temperature** | 83.7 °F (high) / 30 °F (low) |

**Top spot** Belgrade is situated where the Sava and Danube rivers meet. The rivers and their islands offer leisure activities such as swimming and sailing.

**Fact** Belgrade is an eastern Europe information technology center with many international IT companies, like Microsoft and Dell, established here.

**City status**      **National capital**

84

# Ljubljana

## Factfile

| | |
|---|---|
| **Population** | 225,000 |
| **Land area** | 21 square miles |
| **Density** | 10,700 people per square mile |
| **Language** | Slovene |
| **Currency** | Euro |
| **Temperature** | 77 °F (high) / 23 °F (low) |

**Top spot** Looking down on the city is Ljubljana Castle. Built in the 1600s, it has been used as a fortress and barrack, jail, hospital and arsenal.

**Fact** The dragon is the city's symbol and it appears on the flag, coat of arms, a bridge, river walls, manhole covers and on the local soccer team's uniform.

| **City status** | **National capital** |
|---|---|

# Barcelona

## Factfile

| | |
|---|---|
| **Population** | 4,693,000 |
| **Land area** | 415 square miles |
| **Density** | 11,300 people per square mile |
| **Languages** | Spanish and Catalan |
| **Currency** | Euro |
| **Temperature** | 82.4 °F (high) / 39.9 °F (low) |

**Top spot** Sagrada Familia is an unfinished modernist cathedral. The first stone was laid in 1882 and it is hoped that the church will be completed this century!

**Fact** Who founded this city is much debated. Was it Carthaginian troops in 230 BCE or the Greek hero, Hercules, during his search for the Golden Fleece?

**City status**      **Regional capital**

# Stockholm

## Factfile

| | |
|---|---|
| **Population** | 1,484,000 |
| **Land area** | 147 square miles |
| **Density** | 9,300 people per square mile |
| **Language** | Swedish |
| **Currency** | Swedish krona |
| **Temperature** | 70 °F (high) / 20 °F (low) |

**Top spot** Gamla Stan (Old Town) is on an island. It is a well-preserved medieval city and is where Stockholm was founded in 1252. The Royal Palace is here.

**Fact** Stockholm covers 14 islands, and 60 percent of its area is water or parkland. Absence of industry here makes this city one of the world's cleanest.

| **City status** | **National capital** |
|---|---|

87

# Zurich

## Factfile

| | |
|---|---|
| **Population** | 785,000 |
| **Land area** | 95 square miles |
| **Density** | 8,300 people per square mile |
| **Languages** | German, French, Italian and Romansh |
| **Currency** | Swiss franc |
| **Temperature** | 73.9 °F (high) / 28.4 °F (low) |

**Top spot** To know the time in Zurich look up at St. Peterskirche's tower. Each of its four clock faces measure 28 feet across, making them Europe's largest clocks!

**Fact** Regularly listed as one of the world's most livable cities, Zurich is a center for banking. About one-third of its residents do not hold Swiss citizenship.

| **City status** | **Regional capital** |
|---|---|

# Istanbul

## Factfile

| | |
|---|---|
| **Population** | 13,287,000 |
| **Land area** | 525 square miles |
| **Density** | 25,300 people per square mile |
| **Languages** | Turkish (official) and Kurdish |
| **Currency** | Turkish lira |
| **Temperature** | 82.0 °F (high) / 37.0 °F (low) |

**Top spot** Hagia Sophia was a church, a mosque and is now a museum. First built in 360 CE and rebuilt three times, it was the world's largest church for 1,000 years.

**Fact** Istanbul is the only city that sits on two continents: Europe and Asia. It is home to the tulip and to the enormous Grand Bazaar with it 3,000 shops.

| **City status** | **City** |
|---|---|

# Moscow

## Factfile

| | |
|---|---|
| **Population** | 16,170,000 |
| **Land area** | 1,800 square miles |
| **Density** | 9,000 people per square mile |
| **Language** | Russian |
| **Currency** | Russian ruble |
| **Temperature** | 71 °F (high) / 11 °F (low) |

**Top spot** St. Basil's Cathedral is nine colorfully patterned chapels on one foundation. Stalin wanted it demolished as it hindered mass parades on Red Square.

**Fact** Red Square is a significant cultural and political site. St. Basil's, the Kremlin and Senate, and Lenin's Tomb surround it and all main roads run from it.

**City status**          **National capital**

# St. Petersburg

## Factfile

| | |
|---|---|
| **Population** | 5,126,000 |
| **Land area** | 520 square miles |
| **Density** | 9,900 people per square mile |
| **Language** | Russian |
| **Currency** | Russian ruble |
| **Temperature** | 70 °F (high) / 15 °F (low) |

**Top spot** The Winter Palace was the residence of the Russian monarchs until 1917. Today, it is home to the largest art gallery in Russia, the Hermitage.

**Fact** In 1914 the city's name was changed from St. Petersburg to Petrograd, in 1924 to Leningrad, and in 1991 back to the original St. Petersburg!

| City status | City |
|---|---|

# Kiev

## Factfile

| | |
|---|---|
| **Population** | 2,241,000 |
| **Land area** | 210 square miles |
| **Density** | 10,700 people per square mile |
| **Languages** | Ukrainian (official) and Russian |
| **Currency** | Ukrainian hryvnia |
| **Temperature** | 75 °F (high) / 15 °F (low) |

**Top spot** Kiev-Pechersk Lavra (Monastery of the Caves) is now a cluster of gold-domed churches, but the original monastery was in a cave on this site in 1051.

**Fact** The city's name is said to come from Kyi, a founder of the city in 500 CE. Today, Kyiv is the official name. It is Ukraine's largest and richest city.

| City status | National capital |
|---|---|

92

# Edinburgh

## Factfile

| | |
|---|---|
| **Population** | 498,000 |
| **Land area** | 46 square miles |
| **Density** | 9,800 people per square mile |
| **Language** | English |
| **Currency** | Pound sterling |
| **Temperature** | 66.6 °F (high) / 34.0 °F (low) |

**Top spot** Arthur's Seat, part of Holyrood Park, rises 822 feet above Edinburgh and is an extinct volcano. It is an easy and popular walk to the top.

**Fact** The world's largest arts festival, the Edinburgh Festival Fringe, takes place every year in August in 299 venues. The festival was started in 1947.

| City status | Regional capital |
|---|---|

93

# London

## Factfile

| | |
|---|---|
| **Population** | 10,236,000 |
| **Land area** | 671 square miles |
| **Density** | 14,600 people per square mile |
| **Language** | English |
| **Currency** | Pound sterling |
| **Temperature** | 73.2 °F (high) / 33.8 °F (low) |

**Top spot** The Palace of Westminster's tower is often called Big Ben, but Big Ben is the Great Bell inside the clock. The tower is called the Elizabeth Tower.

**Fact** London consists of two ancient cities – the City of London and Westminster. Greater London is the largest capital city in all of Europe.

| City status | National capital |
|---|---|

# Vatican City

## Factfile

| | |
|---|---|
| **Population** | 842 |
| **Land area** | 0.17 square miles |
| **Density** | 4,952 people per square mile |
| **Languages** | Latin (official) and Italian |
| **Currency** | Euro |
| **Temperature** | 83.7 °F (high) / 38.7 °F (low) |

**Top spot** St. Peter's Basilica is the holiest of Catholic shrines as it is built over the tomb of St. Peter. The church is a renowned example of Renaissance architecture.

**Fact** A country within the city of Rome, Vatican City is ruled by the Pope, and is one of the smallest nations in the world. It has its own police force.

**City status**      **City state**

# Montreal

## Factfile

| | |
|---|---|
| **Population** | 3,536,000 |
| **Land area** | 597 square miles |
| **Density** | 5,700 people per square mile |
| **Languages** | French (official) and English |
| **Currency** | Canadian dollar |
| **Temperature** | 80.3 °F (high) / 9.7 °F (low) |

**Top spot** Mount Royal is a park in the center of Montreal Island. Depending on the season, this is the place to cross-country ski, ice skate or just picnic.

**Fact** Montreal is a festival capital. There are festivals for dance, comedy, fashion, circus, music, street art, film and more, with multiple events every month!

| **City status** | **City** |
|---|---|

# Toronto

## Factfile

| | |
|---|---|
| **Population** | 6,456,000 |
| **Land area** | 883 square miles |
| **Density** | 7,300 people per square mile |
| **Languages** | English and French |
| **Currency** | Canadian dollar |
| **Temperature** | 80.7 °F (high) / 13.6 °F (low) |

**Top spot** CN Tower soars 1,815 feet in the air, and offers a hands-free walk outside floor 116. Harnesses and an overhead safety rail keep visitors safe.

**Fact** PATH is Toronto's 19 miles of underground walkway. No matter the weather, people can safely walk to shops, offices, train stations and entertainment.

| City status | Regional capital |
|---|---|

97

# Vancouver

## Factfile

| | |
|---|---|
| **Population** | 2,273,000 |
| **Land area** | 444 square miles |
| **Density** | 4,800 people per square mile |
| **Languages** | English and French |
| **Currency** | Canadian dollar |
| **Temperature** | 71.9 °F (high) / 33.5 °F (low) |

**Top spot** An inukshuk is a marker used by the Inuit. The stone blocks are assembled to have a human shape. It was the logo of the city's Winter Olympics.

**Fact** A makeshift tavern was the only building in the original 1867 settlement, which was named Gastown. This became Granville and then Vancouver.

| City status | City |
|---|---|

# Guatemala City

## Factfile

| | |
|---|---|
| **Population** | 1,289,000 |
| **Land area** | 115 square miles |
| **Density** | 11,200 people per square mile |
| **Languages** | Spanish (official) and Amerindian languages |
| **Currency** | Guatemalan quetzal |
| **Temperature** | 78 °F (high) / 55 °F (low) |

**Top spot** Canopy Zipline is a 1,700-foot glide above and through a rain forest near Guatemala City. The tour ends with an abseil down a 40-foot tree!

**Fact** Nestled between three volcanoes – one still active – this city was a Mayan center. The Mayan people make up over half of the population.

| City status | National capital |
|---|---|

# Tegucigalpa

## Factfile

| | |
|---|---|
| **Population** | 1,120,000 |
| **Land area** | 38 square miles |
| **Density** | 29,500 people per square mile |
| **Languages** | Spanish (official) and Amerindian languages |
| **Currency** | Honduran lempira |
| **Temperature** | 85.0 °F (high) / 59.0 °F (low) |

**Top spot** United Nations National Park, on El Picacho Hill, gives a view of this sprawling city and the damage caused by Hurricane Mitch in 1998.

**Fact** This city, known by the locals as Tegus, is rife with organized crime and gangs. Honduras currently has the highest murder rate in the world.

| City status | National capital |
|---|---|

# Guadalajara

## Factfile

| | |
|---|---|
| **Population** | 4,603,000 |
| **Land area** | 290 square miles |
| **Density** | 15,900 people per square mile |
| **Language** | Spanish |
| **Currency** | Mexican peso |
| **Temperature** | 91.0 °F (high) / 44.0 °F (low) |

**Top spot** Basilica of Our Lady Zapopan is named for a saint who offered protection from storms. The priests' rooms are on two floors alongside the church.

**Fact** Guadalajara is a cultural center and hosts international events. It is most famous as the home of mariachi, a folk music originally played by farmers.

| City status | Regional capital |
|---|---|

101

# Mexico City

## Factfile

| | |
|---|---|
| **Population** | 20,063,000 |
| **Land area** | 800 square miles |
| **Density** | 25,100 people per square mile |
| **Language** | Spanish |
| **Currency** | Mexican peso |
| **Temperature** | 83.5 °F (high) / 42.1 °F (low) |

**Top spot** Metropolitan Cathedral is the largest church in the Americas. Built on soft clay, it is listed as one of the world's 100 Most Endangered Sites.

**Fact** Mexico City – the oldest capital in the Americas – was built on Tenochtitlan, the ancient capital of the Aztecs that was destroyed in 1521.

**City status**      **National capital**

# Managua

## Factfile

| | |
|---|---|
| **Population** | 980,000 |
| **Land area** | 60 square miles |
| **Density** | 16,300 people per square mile |
| **Language** | Spanish |
| **Currency** | Nicaraguan Córdoba |
| **Temperature** | 93.0°F (high) / 70.0 °F (low) |

**Top spot**  Acahualinca on Lake Managua is where 2,120-year-old fossil footprints of 15 humans were uncovered. It is a site of great scientific importance.

**Fact**  Managua's economy is based mainly on trade. The city is Nicaragua's chief trading center for coffee, cotton, melons, and other crops.

| **City status** | **National capital** |
|---|---|

103

# Boston

## Factfile

| | |
|---|---|
| **Population** | 4,478,000 |
| **Land area** | 2,056 square miles |
| **Density** | 2,100 people per square mile |
| **Language** | English |
| **Currency** | United States dollar |
| **Temperature** | 81.6 °F (high) / 22.2 °F (low) |

**Top spot** Fenway Park is the home of the Boston Red Sox baseball team. Opened in 1912, it is the oldest and most historic ballpark in Major League Baseball.

**Fact** On September 1, 1897, the first subway in the US opened in Boston. On that day, 100,000 people took the short ride on the Tremont Street Subway.

| **City status** | **Regional capital** |
|---|---|

# Chicago

## Factfile

| | |
|---|---|
| **Population** | 9,156,000 |
| **Land area** | 2,647 square miles |
| **Density** | 3,400 people per square mile |
| **Language** | English |
| **Currency** | United States dollar |
| **Temperature** | 84.1 °F (high) / 16.5 °F (low) |

**Top spot** Willis Tower, or Sears Tower, is 1,451 feet high and for 25 years was the world's tallest building. It is the city's most popular tourist destination.

**Fact** Chicago is known for its museums. The Field Museum of Natural History is home to the world's most complete fossil skeleton of a Tyrannosaurus rex.

| **City status** | **City** |
|---|---|

105

# Dallas

## Factfile

| | |
|---|---|
| **Population** | 6,174,000 |
| **Land area** | 1,998 square miles |
| **Density** | 2,800 people per square mile |
| **Language** | English |
| **Currency** | United States dollar |
| **Temperature** | 96.1 °F (high) / 35.5 °F (low) |

**Top spot** The AT&T Stadium, home to the Dallas Cowboys football team, is so huge that the Statue of Liberty would fit comfortably inside it!

**Fact** Dallas is known for its historical association with the oil and cotton industries. It is also where President John F. Kennedy was shot in 1963.

| **City status** | **City** |
|---|---|

# Las Vegas

## Factfile

| | |
|---|---|
| **Population** | 2,191,000 |
| **Land area** | 417 square miles |
| **Density** | 4,500 people per square mile |
| **Language** | English |
| **Currency** | United States dollar |
| **Temperature** | 104.2 °F (high) / 38.7 °F (low) |

**Top spot** Each year 41 million people visit this casino city, staying in its many famous hotels. Seventeen of the nation's 20 biggest hotels are in Las Vegas.

**Fact** Las Vegas is situated in the Mojave Desert and is surrounded by mountain ranges that act as barriers to rain-bearing clouds. It is sunny 310 days a year!

| City status | City |
|---|---|

# Los Angeles

## Factfile

| | |
|---|---|
| **Population** | 15,058,000 |
| **Land area** | 2,432 square miles |
| **Density** | 6,000 people per square mile |
| **Language** | English |
| **Currency** | United States dollar |
| **Temperature** | 83.1 °F (high) / 48.3 °F (low) |

**Top spot** Hollywood is the center of the motion picture industry. Over 2,500 brass and terrazzo stars mark the Walk of Fame to honor cinema's greatest stars.

**Fact** The Los Angeles area was claimed for the Spanish Empire in 1542, but its first Mexican settlers are honored on Olvera Street, the oldest part of LA.

| City status | City |
|---|---|

# Miami

## Factfile

**Population**   5,764,000
**Land area**   1,239 square miles
**Density**   4,400 people per square mile
**Language**   English
**Currency**   United States dollar
**Temperature**   91 °F (high) / 59.9 °F (low)

**Top spot**   Freedom Tower, built as a newspaper office, gained its name in the 1960s when it became a processing center for refugees fleeing Castro's Cuba.

**Fact**   Miami is a tropical playground with 15 award-winning beaches, over 80 parks and scores of golf courses. There is also sailing, fishing and diving.

| City status | City |
| --- | --- |

## Factfile

| | |
|---|---|
| **Population** | 922,000 |
| **Land area** | 251 square miles |
| **Density** | 3,600 people per square mile |
| **Language** | English |
| **Currency** | United States dollar |
| **Temperature** | 90.9 °F (high) / 43.2 °F (low) |

**Top spot** The French Quarter with its Jackson Square is a lively, noisy place. The sound of jazz and blues fills the air, especially during Mardi Gras.

**Fact** This city is circled by water and much of the city is built on wetlands, making it flood prone, which almost stopped the French from settling here.

| City status | City |
|---|---|

# New York

## Factfile

| | |
|---|---|
| **Population** | 20,630,000 |
| **Land area** | 4,495 square miles |
| **Density** | 4,500 people per square mile |
| **Language** | English |
| **Currency** | United States dollar |
| **Temperature** | 85.3 °F (high) / 26.6 °F (low) |

**Top spot** The Statue of Liberty was gifted to NY in 1886 by the people of France as a symbol of freedom. It is on Liberty Island and the copper statue is 151 feet tall.

**Fact** New York is the most populated city in the US, and is made up of five areas (boroughs): the Bronx, Manhattan, Queens, Brooklyn and Staten Island.

| **City status** | **City** |
|---|---|

111

# Philadelphia

## Factfile

| | |
|---|---|
| **Population** | 5,570,000 |
| **Land area** | 1,981 square miles |
| **Density** | 2,700 people per square mile |
| **Language** | English |
| **Currency** | United States dollar |
| **Temperature** | 87.1 °F (high) / 25.6 °F (low) |

**Top spot** In Independence Hall the Declaration of Independence and the Constitution were debated and adopted in 1776 and 1787 respectively.

**Fact** The founder of Philadelphia, William Penn, designed the city using a grid to create blocks of buildings. This design has been used by many US cities.

| City status | City |
|---|---|

# San Francisco

## Factfile

| | |
|---|---|
| **Population** | 5,929,000 |
| **Land area** | 1,080 square miles |
| **Density** | 5,400 people per square mile |
| **Language** | English |
| **Currency** | United States dollar |
| **Temperature** | 69.8 °F (high) / 45.6 °F (low) |

**Top spot** The Golden Gate Bridge, possibly the most photographed bridge in the world, is painted orange to give it visibility during the city's frequent fogs.

**Fact** This city runs along the Pacific Ocean and around San Francisco Bay, and has 50 hills and six islands. Alcatraz Island was until 1963 an infamous jail.

| City status | City |
|---|---|

113

# Seattle

## Factfile

**Population** 3,128,000
**Land area** 1,010 square miles
**Density** 3,000 people per square mile
**Language** English
**Currency** United States dollar
**Temperature** 76.3 °F (high) / 35.6 °F (low)

**Top spot** The Space Needle began as a doodle on a napkin and became Seattle's futuristic landmark. Completed in 1961 for the World's Fair, it is 605 feet tall.

**Fact** Seattle, once a logging town, is now associated with aircraft manufacture and technology. Both Boeing and Amazon started in Seattle.

| City status | City |
| --- | --- |

# Washington, DC

## Factfile

| | |
|---|---|
| **Population** | 4,889,000 |
| **Land area** | 1,322 square miles |
| **Density** | 3,500 people per square mile |
| **Language** | English |
| **Currency** | United States dollar |
| **Temperature** | 88.4 °F (high) / 28.6 °F (low) |

**Top spot** Capitol Hill is one of the oldest parts of Washington, DC. Though mostly residential, the workplace of the Congress – the US Capitol – is here.

**Fact** Washington, DC is the capital of the US. The President's residence, the White House, and the Lincoln Memorial and the Pentagon are in this city.

| **City status** | **National capital** |
|---|---|

# Buenos Aires

## Factfile

| | |
|---|---|
| **Population** | 14,122,000 |
| **Land area** | 1,035 square miles |
| **Density** | 13,600 people per square mile |
| **Language** | Spanish |
| **Currency** | Argentine peso |
| **Temperature** | 86.7 °F (high) / 45.3 °F (low) |

**Top spot** La Casa Rosada is the office of Argentina's President. It was painted pink to satisfy both the "white" political party and the opposing "red" party.

**Fact** Avenida 9 de Julio is the widest street in the world. It has a staggering 16 lanes of traffic. To cross this road requires at least two sets of traffic lights.

| **City status** | **National capital** |
|---|---|

116

# Santa Cruz de la Sierra

## Factfile

| | |
|---|---|
| **Population** | 2,110,000 |
| **Land area** | 230 square miles |
| **Density** | 9,200 people per square mile |
| **Languages** | Spanish, Quechua and Aymara |
| **Currency** | Bolivian boliviano |
| **Temperature** | 86 °F (high) / 62 °F (low) |

**Top spot** Fuerte de Samaipata has been occupied since 300 CE by many cultures, including Aztec and Inca. This archaeological site is World Heritage listed.

**Fact** Up until 60 years ago, Santa Cruz was a small town. Since the 1950s it has grown to become one of the fastest-growing cities in the world.

| City status | Regional capital |
|---|---|

# Rio de Janeiro

## Factfile

| | |
|---|---|
| **Population** | 11,727,000 |
| **Land area** | 780 square miles |
| **Density** | 15,000 people per square mile |
| **Languages** | Portuguese (official) and Spanish |
| **Currency** | Brazilian real |
| **Temperature** | 91.2 °F (high) / 62.4 °F (low) |

**Top spot**
Christ the Redeemer statue looks down onto the city from atop a 2,300-foot mountain. It is 98 feet tall and its arms are 92 feet from tip to tip.

**Fact**
Rio was founded in 1565 by a Portuguese explorer. In 2015, the people celebrated the city's 450th birthday with a giant 3,000-egg birthday cake.

| City status | National capital |
|---|---|

# São Paulo

## Factfile

| | |
|---|---|
| **Population** | 20,365,000 |
| **Land area** | 1,045 square miles |
| **Density** | 19,500 people per square mile |
| **Languages** | Portuguese (official) and Spanish |
| **Currency** | Brazilian real |
| **Temperature** | 83 °F (high) / 55 °F (low) |

**Top spot** Theatro Municipal's decorated and colorful facade is a mix of many different styles. Its interior, clad in gold and marble, is a feast for the eyes!

**Fact** São Paulo is one of the world's most densely populated cities. Friday evening traffic jams heading out of the city can be over 110 miles long!

| **City status** | **Regional capital** |
|---|---|

119

# Santiago

## Factfile

| | |
|---|---|
| **Population** | 6,225,000 |
| **Land area** | 380 square miles |
| **Density** | 16,400 people per square mile |
| **Language** | Spanish |
| **Currency** | Chilean peso |
| **Temperature** | 85 °F (high) / 37 °F (low) |

**Top spot** Palacio de la Moneda, now the office of Chile's President, was the mint ("moneda" is a coin). The changing of the guard is done with much ceremony.

**Fact** Santiago is on the Pacific Ring of Fire, an area of volcanoes and seismic activity. In 2010 it was hit by the sixth-largest earthquake ever recorded.

**City status**      **National capital**

# Bogotá

## Factfile

| | |
|---|---|
| **Population** | 8,991,000 |
| **Land area** | 190 square miles |
| **Density** | 47,300 people per square mile |
| **Language** | Spanish |
| **Currency** | Colombian peso |
| **Temperature** | 67 °F (high) / 45 °F (low) |

**Top spot** Monserrate is a 10,241-foot mountain that dominates the center of the city and affords great views. The church at the summit is a pilgrim destination.

**Fact** This city, cradled in the Andes Mountains, is a mix of colonial mansions and shiny high-rises, rich and poor, traditional culture and the very new.

**City status**      **National capital**

# Quito

## Factfile

| | |
|---|---|
| **Population** | 1,720,000 |
| **Land area** | 185 square miles |
| **Density** | 9,300 people per square mile |
| **Languages** | Spanish (official) and Amerindian languages |
| **Currency** | United States dollar |
| **Temperature** | 68 °F (high) / 49 °F (low) |

**Top spot** Basilica del Voto Nacional has carvings of native animals like iguanas. It is unfinished since legend says the world will end when the church is completed.

**Fact** Quito was built on the ruins of an ancient Inca city. It is 9,350 feet above sea level, making it the second-highest capital city in the world.

| City status | National capital |
|---|---|

# Lima

## Factfile

| | |
|---|---|
| **Population** | 10,750,000 |
| **Land area** | 355 square miles |
| **Density** | 30,300 people per square mile |
| **Languages** | Spanish and Quechua |
| **Currency** | Peruvian nuevo sol |
| **Temperature** | 80 °F (high) / 59 °F (low) |

**Top spot** The Monastery of San Francisco boasts macabre catacombs. They were discovered in 1943, and contain the decorated bones of over 25,000 people.

**Fact** Lima is a busy city where a quarter of the population of Peru live. The city sprawl is so large, the locals nicknamed Lima "The Octopus."

| City status | National capital |
|---|---|

123

# Montevideo

## Factfile

| | |
|---|---|
| **Population** | 1,700,000 |
| **Land area** | 100 square miles |
| **Density** | 17,000 people per square mile |
| **Language** | Spanish |
| **Currency** | Uruguayan peso |
| **Temperature** | 83 °F (high) / 43 °F (low) |

**Top spot** Pocitos Beach is one of many beaches on the city's 17-mile "Rambla." This pedestrian avenue runs the length of Montevideo's Altantic coast.

**Fact** Montevideo holds the longest carnival in the world – it lasts 40 noisy days! The city has a museum dedicated to its 100-year-old carnival history.

| City status | National capital |
|---|---|

# Caracas

## Factfile

| | |
|---|---|
| **Population** | 2,861,000 |
| **Land area** | 114 square miles |
| **Density** | 25,100 people per square mile |
| **Language** | Spanish |
| **Currency** | Venezuelan bolívar |
| **Temperature** | 82 °F (high) / 63 °F (low) |

**Top spot** Plaza Bolivar in the city's historic center honors Simón Bolívar, a hero who gained Venezuela's independence from Spanish rule in 1821.

**Fact** Built in a narrow valley between two densely forested mountain ranges, Caracas is often shrouded in a dense fog that the locals call "Pacheco."

| **City status** | **National capital** |
|---|---|

125

# Glossary

**Altitude** The vertical height of an object measured from sea level or ground level.

**Amphitheater** An open circular or oval building with a central space for performances.

**Ancestors** People who were in your family in past times.

**Ancient** Belonging to, or coming from, a time that was long ago.

**Apartheid** A former social system in South Africa in which black people and people from other racial groups did not have the same rights as white people.

**Aztecs** The Native South American people who ruled Mexico and neighboring areas before the 16th century Spanish conquest.

**Basilica** A church that is given special privileges by the Pope as head of the Catholic Church.

**Buddhist** A person who follows the religious teachings of Buddha.

**Capital** A city that is the official seat of government in a political entity, such as a state or nation.

**Carthaginians** People from the ancient city and state of Carthage in northern Africa.

**Catacomb** An underground cemetery consisting of chambers or tunnels with recesses for graves.

**Cathedral** The principal church of a district, containing the bishop's official throne.

**Christian** A member of a Christian church.

**Civilization** A stage of human social development and organization that is considered most advanced.

**Colonial** A style of architecture imported by a ruling power into another country.

**Commercial** Concerned with or engaged in making profit.

**Continent** A continuous expanse of land that may contain nations.

**Cosmopolitan** A city that has people or elements from all parts of the world.

**Cultural** The arts and intellectual achievements of a people or place.

**Democracy** A government where the people take part in governing.

**Legislative** Having the power to make laws.

**Economy** The system of how money is made and used within a particular country or region.

**Empire** A group of countries under a single authority.

**Ethnic** People of the same race or nationality who share a distinctive culture.

**Financial** The management of money, credit and banking.

**Hindu** A follower of the religion of Hinduism.

**Iconic** Something widely recognized and well established.

**Imperial** Relating to an empire or an emperor.

**Incas** The Quechuan people of Peru who ruled until the Spanish conquest in the 16th century.

**Independence** Freedom from outside control or support.

**Inuit** A group of culturally similar indigenous people inhabiting the Arctic regions of Greenland, Canada, and Alaska.

**Islamic** Relating to the religion of Islam.

**Jew** Someone whose religion is Judaism, who is descended from Jewish people, or who participates in the culture surrounding Judaism.

**Landmark** An object or structure that is easy to see and recognize.

**Mausoleum** A building that houses a tomb or group of tombs.

**Medieval** A period from the 5th–15th century in Europe.

**Merchant** A person or company involved in trade, especially with foreign countries.

**Monastery** A building or buildings that were occupied by monks living under religious vows.

**Monument** A statue, building, or structure erected to commemorate a notable person or event.

**Mosque** A Muslim place of worship.

**Phoenicians** A member of a Semitic people inhabiting ancient Phoenicia (now Syria and Lebanon) and its colonies.

**Refugee** A person forced to leave his/her country to escape war, persecution, or natural disaster.

**Renaissance** A cultural and artistic style that was developed in Europe in the 14th–16th centuries.

**Republic** A country with elected representatives and an elected head of state who is usually a president, rather than a monarch.

**Temple** A building devoted to the worship of a god or gods.

**World Heritage Site** A natural or man-made area or structure that is of outstanding importance. World Heritage status is awarded by the United Nations Educational, Scientific and Cultural Organization (UNESCO).

# Index